Fox and Dog

Written by Charlotte Raby

Illustrated by James Cottell

Collins

red fox
• • • • • •

Jet the dog

red fox

Jet the dog

red fox on a van

the dog yaps

red fox on a van

the dog yaps

fox zig zags off

wet dog

fox zig zags off

wet dog

🐾 Review: After reading 🐾

Use your assessment from hearing the children read to choose any GPCs, words or tricky words that need additional practice.

Read 1: Decoding

- Read the whole book to the children and ask them to follow.
- Turn to page 10 and ask the children to read the text. Ask if they can hear that the "z" and the "s" both make a /z/ sound.

Read 2: Vocabulary

- Go back through the book and discuss the pictures. Encourage children to talk about details that stand out for them. Use a dialogic talk model to expand on their ideas and recast them in full sentences as naturally as possible.
- Work together to expand vocabulary by naming objects in the pictures that children do not know.
- Ask: Does the fox walk off in a straight line at the end of the story? How do you know? (*No, the story says fox "zig zags" which means fox moves side to side or in a wavy line.*)

Read 3: Comprehension

- Turn to pages 14 and 15.
  - o Ask: Who are the main characters in the story? (*red fox and Jet the dog*)
  - o Encourage children to talk about what happened in the story using the picture as a reminder (e.g. *the footprints on the van, the pond, etc*).
- Encourage the children to make connections from their own lives and what they may have seen or experienced with what they have seen in the book. Ask: Have you ever seen a fox? Where was it? What was it doing?